From PRISON to Promise

AN OVERVIEW OF EXODUS, LEVITICUS, NUMBERS, AND DEUTERONOMY

JACK HAYFORD
SCOTT BAUER • JACK HAMILTON

FROM PRISON TO PROMISE
A Practical, Introductory Guidebook for a Comprehensive Overview in the Bible Books of EXODUS, LEVITICUS, NUMBERS, and DEUTERONOMY

Photographs of Dr. Jack Hayford, Dr. Scott Bauer, and Dr. Jack Hamilton by Christopher Glenn Photography.

Published by Living Way Ministries
14300 Sherman Way
Van Nuys, CA (USA) 91405-2499
(818) 779-8400 • (800) 776-8180

ISBN 0-916847-21-7
Printed in the United States of America

Table of Contents

GROWING WITH THE BIBLE BOOK-A-MONTH STUDIES

Disciples of the Lord Jesus Christ know it: *There is no substitute for the Word of God in our daily lives!* Still, many find that the formation of a satisfying, fulfilling discipline in reading and studying God's Word is not easy. In contrast, many fall into a merely regimented or legalistic habit that eventually withers for lack of the Holy Spirit's breath upon it. Others have difficulty finding direction or maintaining focus; besides, we all need help to keep us moving forward *through* the Word.

The formulation of the "Bible Book-A-Month" concept was born in the heart of Dr. Jack Hayford, who, as a pastor, constantly seeks improved means of helping people achieve three things: *systematic, substantial,* and *thorough* coverage of the Bible. Each is important to accomplish the objective of good Bible study, and they can be realized through this plan.

(1) It's <u>systematic</u>, by reason of the *month-by-month* advancement of the program; (2) it's <u>substantial</u>, because of the *spiritual weight* of the triangular

approach of study employed; and (3) it's thorough, for *every book* of the Bible is incorporated in it.

THE TRIANGULAR APPROACH

There are many worthwhile approaches to a study of the Holy Bible. For example, "synthetic" study—which draws together highlights to provide a quick grasp of a book; "critical" study—which assesses the ancient textual resources that authenticate the trustworthiness of the book as a document; or "verse-by-verse" study—which seeks to exhaust every book of the totality of its content.

Distinct from any of these, the "Bible Book-A-Month" study seeks to achieve the maximum possible grasp of a book's truth while keeping a pace forward which sustains the average Bible student's interest. It is demanding enough in its *academics* to seriously engage those interested in intelligent, thought-provoking study. Yet it is dynamic enough in its *movement* to avoid losing passion, and to keep each student at a point of continuous anticipation. This is done through use of a **"triangular approach"** to each book—which focuses the three primary things to be found in every book of the Bible.

1. Each Bible book contains an *essential message*: the core concepts which distinguish that book and provide its place in God's Word. This is found in *towering truths* and *pillar passages* within that book. These together provide a rich overview of the Holy Spirit's theme and thrust in that book of the Bible.

2. Each Bible book presents *problems* and evokes *questions* rising from the need to integrate that book's content with the whole Bible, as well as to interpret its content as it addresses current issues. Good Bible study helps questioners find *satisfactory answers* to reasoned inquiry, even as it demonstrates the *relevancy* of God's Word to today's social problems. Thus, we discover the power of the Holy Spirit—present to reveal Christ to the world—TODAY!

3. Each Bible book provides *practical wisdom* and *personal guidance*; it sheds light on the believer's daily walk and service as he or she follows Jesus Christ. Healthy study in God's Word should provide *information* and *inspiration*, but only as it issues in *incarnation* does it achieve its goal! In each book, *insights for faithful, fruitful pathways* will show how to adopt, adapt, and apply the Bible to your life, as Jesus' disciple.

These perspectives provide the viewpoints which "triangulate" on the text: each book studied through three lessons which unfold the truth of God's Word noting one of the above three values. The "Bible Book-A-Month" triangular approach works this way:

- Dr. Jack Hayford's presentation is first, providing a full picture of the purpose and message of each book.

- Dr. Scott Bauer's lesson is second, affording a grasp of the relevancy of each book and revealing the Spirit's power as it unveils Jesus Himself.

- Dr. Jack Hamilton's lesson is third in each volume, presenting the practical lessons of each book.

By means of these three lessons, a comprehensive overview of a book (or books) of the Bible is presented in each study, so it can be truly gained, grasped, and applied.

TRIPLE TOOLS—SUPPORT RESOURCES

1. Each Bible book, and the studies as originally presented, will be available on audio cassettes. Because Pastor Hayford has been asked by a national distributor of audio Bibles to record the whole of the Scriptures in the New King James Version, the text being studied is on tape. These audio Bibles are being produced now, and each correlated reading will be released in conjunction with the "Bible Book-A-Month" program (Fall 1996 through Spring 1998).
2. Audio cassettes of the three lessons are also available with each study guide. These contain the complete teachings by Drs. Hayford, Bauer, and Hamilton and will become available as they are produced from month to month.
3. The above two join with the entire set of books (like this one) to complete the support resources for the "Bible Book-A-Month" studies. Additional resources, noted in each volume, may also be ordered by calling Living Way Ministries at 800-776-8180.

	EXODUS	LEVITICUS	NUMBERS	DEUTERONOMY
KEY WORD	REDEMPTION	HOLINESS	WANDERINGS	COVENANT
KEY CHAPTERS	EXODUS 12-14	LEVITICUS 16	NUMBERS 14	DEUTERONOMY 27
KEY VERSES	**EXODUS 19:5-6** *"…if you will indeed obey My voice and keep My covenant, then you shall be a special treasure to Me above all people… And you shall be to me a kingdom of priests and a holy nation."*	**LEVITICUS 20:7-8** *"Consecrate yourselves therefore, and be holy, for I am the Lord your God. And you shall keep my statutes, and perform them: I am the Lord who sanctifies you."*	**NUMBERS 20:12** *"Then the Lord spoke to Moses and Aaron, "Because you did not believe me, to hallow Me in the eyes of the children of Israel, therefore you shall not bring this assembly into the land which I have given them."*	**DEUTERONOMY 30:19-20** *"…I have set before you life and death, blessing and cursing; therefore choose life, that both you and your descendants may live; that you may love the Lord your God, that you may obey His voice, and that you may cling to Him, for He is your life and the length of your days…"*

Introducing the Bible Books of
EXODUS, LEVITICUS, NUMBERS, AND DEUTERONOMY

Author:	Traditionally, Moses
Dates:	About 1400 to 1445 B.C.
Themes:	Deliverance, The Sanctity of God and Holiness in Everyday Life, Yahweh's Guiding Presence, Obedience Brings Blessing, Disobedience Cursing
Key Words:	Deliver, Sacrifice, Sign, Tabernacle, Sanctuary, Holiness, Offering, Sacrifice,Census, Murmuring, Purity, Tabernacle of Meeting, Covenant, Obey, Blessed, Cursed

Author

The books of Exodus, Leviticus, Numbers, and Deuteronomy are all attributed to Moses, the Hebrew prophet who led the Israelites out of Egypt. Through various events and face-to-face encounters with God, Moses received the revelation of those things God wanted to be known. Then, through the process of Holy Spirit inspiration, Moses communicated this revealed information to the Hebrew people both orally and in written form. The last chapter of Deuteronomy, which contains the account of Moses' death, was probably written by his intimate friend Joshua.

Date

Conservative tradition dates Moses' death sometime around 1400 B.C., so these books were likely written during the forty years preceding it. Deuteronomy covers less than a two-month period, which includes the thirty days of mourning for Moses' death.

An Outline of

EXODUS

I.	**The miraculous deliverance of Israel**	**1:1-13:16**
A.	Oppression of the Israelites in Egypt	1:1-22
B.	The birth and early life of Moses	2:1-4:31
C.	The deliverance process	5:1-11:10
D.	The Exodus event	12:1-13:16
II.	**The miraculous journey to Sinai**	**13:17-18:27**
A.	Deliverance at the Red Sea	13:17-15:21
B.	Provisions provided	15:22-17:7
C.	Protection from Amalekites	17:8-16
D.	Establishment of ruling elders	18:1-27
III.	**The miraculous revelations at Sinai**	**19:1-40:38**
A.	Arrival at Sinai and God's appearing	19:1-25
B.	The Ten Commandments	20:1-21
C.	The Book of the Covenant	20:22-23:19
D.	God's Angel of protection	23:20-33
E.	Israel accepts the covenant	24:1-18
F.	Directions concerning the tabernacle	25:1-31:18
G.	The golden calf	32:1-35
H.	Repentance and renewal of covenant	33:1-35:3
I.	Building the tabernacle	35:4-40:33
J.	The glory of the Lord filling the tabernacle	40:34-38

An Outline of
LEVITICUS

I.	**The description of the sacrificial system**	**1:1-7:38**
	A. The burnt offering	1:1-17
	B. The grain offering	2:1-16
	C. The peace offering	3:1-17
	D. The sin offering	4:1-5:13
	E. The trespass offering	5:14-6:7
	F. Other instructions	6:8-7:38
II.	**The service of the priests in the sanctuary**	**8:1-10:20**
	A. Ordination of Aaron and his sons	8:1-36
	B. The priests take office	9:1-24
	C. The sin of Nadab and Abihu	10:1-11
	D. The sin of Eleazar and Ithamar	10:12-20
III.	**The laws of impurities**	**11:1-16:34**
	A. Animal impurities	11:1-47
	B. Childbirth impurities	12:1-8
	C. Skin impurities	13:1-14:57
	D. Discharge impurities	15:1-33
	E. Moral impurities	16:1-34
IV.	**The holiness code**	**17:1-26:46**
	A. Killing for food	17:1-16
	B. On being holy	18:1-20:27
	C. Laws for priests and sacrifices	21:1-22:33
	D. Holy days and religious feasts	23:1-44
	E. Laws for holy elements of worship	24:1-9
	F. Punishment for blasphemy	24:10-23

	G. The Sabbath and the Jubilee years	25:1-55
	H. Blessing for obedience and punishment for disobedience	26:1-46
V.	**Gifts to the sanctuary**	**27:1-34**

AN OUTLINE OF NUMBERS

I.	**Instructions for the journey from Sinai**	**1:1-10:10**
	A. Account of census taking	1:1-4:49
	B. Further instructions and accounts	5:1-10:10
II.	**Account of the journey from Sinai**	**10:11-36:13**
	A. Rebellion and punishment of first generation	10:11-25:18
	B. Preparation of the new generation	26:1-36:13

AN OUTLINE OF DEUTERONOMY

I.	**Moses' first message**	**1:1-4:43**
	A. Introduction	1:1-5
	B. The Past remembered	1:6-3:29
	C. A call of obedience	4:1-40
	D. Cities of refuge appointed	4:41-43
II.	**Moses' second message**	**4:44-26:19**
	A. Exposition of the Ten Commandments	4:44-11:32

B. Exposition of the ceremonial laws 12:1-16:17
C. Exposition of the civil law 16:18-18:22
D. Exposition of the criminal laws 19:1-21:9
E. Exposition of the social laws 21:10-26:19

III. Moses' third message 27:1-30:20
A. Ratification ceremony 27:1-26
B. Covenant sanctions 28:1-68
C. The covenant oath 29:1-30:20

IV. Moses' final words and death 31:1-34:12
A. Perpetuation of the covenant 31:1-29
B. The song of witness 31:30-32:47
C. Moses' blessing on Israel 32:48-33:29
D. Moses' death and successor 34:1-12

THE EXODUS FROM
EGYPT

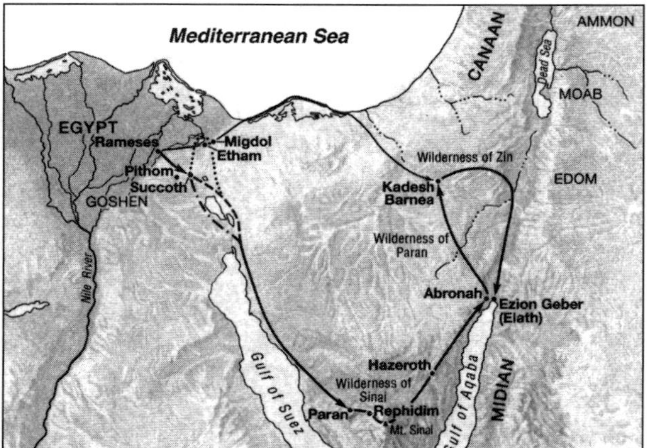

Nelson's Complete Book of Maps and Charts © 1993, Thomas Nelson, Inc.

PART 1

THE PILLAR PRINCIPLES OF EXODUS, LEVITICUS, NUMBERS, AND DEUTERONOMY

JACK HAYFORD

When the Events in EXODUS, NUMBERS, and DEUTERONOMY Occurred

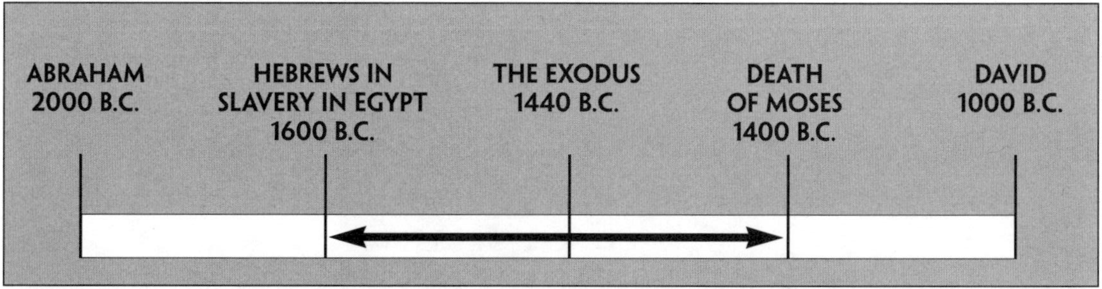

EXODUS records the miraculous: deliverance of Israel, journey to Sinai, and revelation at Sinai. NUMBERS tells how the Lord corrects and guides His redeemed toward fulfilling His purposes. DEUTERONOMY is a plea to obey God based upon the twin motives of love and fear.

THE PILLAR PRINCIPLES OF EXODUS THROUGH DEUTERONOMY

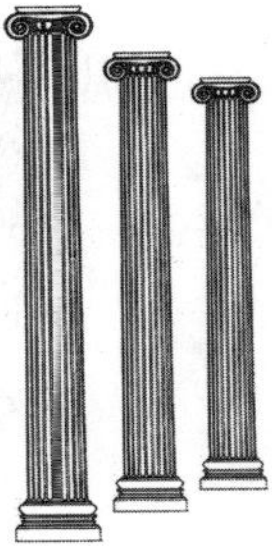

From the rocky shores of the Red Sea to the milk-and-honey dream of a Promised Land, God took a people—ages ago. He manifested a power and might—beginning with the unexplainable but prophetic power of the blood of a lamb struck over the doorpost of a household. He bought a people, then He *brought* His people, and the whole of this magnificent story might be summed up in four words: **"From Prison to Promise!"**

We begin a study of four great books, Exodus through Deuteronomy, which follow Genesis' "beginnings" with three primary features constituting their pages. These four remaining books of the Pentateuch (the five books of Moses, commonly called *The Torah*) intersperse three things:

THE UNFOLDING STORY: Contained for the most part in approximately 40 chapters—Exodus 1-20, and 40, with Numbers 9-25, and 36. While an episode or two crops up elsewhere, this is the body of the narrative—from Egypt to the edge of Canaan.

THE WORSHIP-PLACE: Building the Tabernacle and establishing the order of worship was God's priority for Israel's coming to know Him. Exodus 21-39 essentially is dedicated to giving the pattern for an earthly place of worship.

THE WORSHIP-PLAN: Leviticus joins to Exodus to mark out the offerings and the feasts God's people were to celebrate. It also points to the practical patterns of purity they were to observe for their health, and the moral practices they were to observe for their own benefit and as an appropriate response to the Holy One who had delivered them.

There are other issues—notably, the taking of the census of the people at the end of the 40 years in the wilderness, and the registering of what the geographic boundaries should be for each of the various tribes. But for our purpose in examining the primary concepts in these pages which record Israel's deliverance from Egypt and her wilderness journeys, we will draw on the above three issues and elaborate three great themes:

Undergirding Concepts, which are threaded through the whole of the text and which help us unto grand and embracing points of understanding.

Pictures of Christ, which are woven through the fabric of the works and worship of God as He brings His people out to bring His people in.

Timeless Lessons for Life, which spring from the pages to speak prophetically today, saying, *"All that happened then is for now!"*

I. UNDERGIRDING CONCEPTS

A. God's Covenants With Israel

One of the most challenging points in understanding the Bible as it discusses God's ancient people, the Jews, is to discern the Apostle Paul's words in Romans, chapters 9-11. He carefully distinguishes there (as well as in Galatians 3 and Romans 4) that there is a difference between Abraham's biological and spiritual offspring. The *natural seed* is the Hebrew peoples—national Israel; a people to whom He revealed Himself in special ways, and with whom He still has special purposes yet to be fulfilled. The *spiritual seed* is the Church—both Jews and Gentiles who have received Jesus as the Messiah—the Savior.

In Romans 9, Paul says of national Israel, *"Israelites, to whom pertain the adoption, the glory, the covenants, the giving of the law, the service of God, and the promises, of whom are the fathers and from whom, according to the flesh, Christ came, who is over all, the eternally blessed God. Amen"* (verses 4-5).

It is significant that most of the God-given graces mentioned in this text were given in the portion of God's Word before us: (a) the adoption—Exodus 19:5; (b) the glory—Exodus 40:34; (c) the giving of the law—Exodus 20:1-17; (d) the service (i.e., worship) of God—Exodus 25-39, in the Tabernacle; (e) the promises—abounding throughout (example, Exodus 15:26; 17:15-16), but crystallized in the classic "blessings" passage—Deuteronomy 28:1-14).

God made a promise of "the land" to Abraham and his natural seed, and He gave the sign of circumcision as a confirmation of his faith. Those, joined to the above, are cited by Paul in the New Testament, and he reminds us that God has not forgotten any of this. That *The Church*—Abraham's "spiritual seed"—is the primary means of achieving His redemptive purposes on earth today is unquestioned. But that He has made commitments to Abraham's "natural seed" should remain equally unquestioned.

B. These Episodes Are for NOW!

It is always wise to remember the general principle that the Bible is meant to be applied. But there are New Testament passages which especially call our attention to a key concept: these episodes are especially applicable!

1 Corinthians 10 elaborates details of Israel's wilderness journey. It issues this summons: *"Now all these things happened to them as examples, and they were written for our admonition, upon whom the ends of the ages have come. Therefore let him who thinks he stands take heed lest he fall"* (verses 11-12).

Romans 15:4 brings home a very similar point: *"For whatever things were written before were written for our learning, that we through the patience and comfort of the Scriptures might have hope."*

The majority of the Book of Hebrews develops features of both: Israel's journey (chapter 4), and features of Israel's worship (chapters 7-10) to exhort us and call us to (a) be warned against apathy and (b) be strengthened through the assurance that is ours in Christ.

C. Faithful Worship Gains God's Presence

The heart of God's desire to abide among His people—then and now—is tenderly disclosed as He prefaces His call to build the Tabernacle: *"Let them make Me a sanctuary, that I may dwell among them... And there I will meet with you and I will speak with you from above the mercy seat"* (Exodus 25:8, 22).

In directing the erecting of that Tabernacle, a principle is laid down: *It is not the privilege of man to dictate the terms of God's presence.* So repeatedly the Lord says, "Make it according to the pattern I have given" (Exodus 25:9, 40; 26:30; 27:8). When that had faithfully been done (Exodus 39:32, 42), the wonder of His presence was the gracious reward of obedience in worship—His arrival in *glory!* (Exodus 40:34, 35).

This is a timeless concept for application, just as the New Testament teaches us in Romans 12:1-2.

To worship as Jesus said (John 4:24, "in Spirit and in truth") we are called to present our total beings—body, soul, mind and spirit. We are *not* to govern our worship by the mood, acceptance, or standards of the world—*"be not conformed!"*

It is humble, childlike, obedient worship that gains the joyous blessing of "seasons of refreshing from the presence of the Lord" (Acts 4:19), and which realizes the "rain" of divine grace (Zechariah 14:17) when God is approached with living worship "according to the pattern."

D. God Calls His People Unto Holiness

From the confused existence of an enslaved people unto the ordered lifestyle of a people of destiny,

Israel was called. The multitudinous regulations and mandates contained in the code of God's ordinances were not meaningless religious strictures. Throughout the pages of Leviticus, scattered through Exodus and Numbers, then reviewed in detail in Deuteronomy, God sets forth requirements—"because the Lord your God is holy."

God's purpose for holiness is redemptive, not restrictive. The directives issued are intended to maintain physical health, sustain social well-being, and advance practical wholeness in all of life. In the third section of this study guide ("Holy Living in a Profane World"), you will find the "live-ability" of God's laws is elaborated, with a special focus on the Book of Leviticus.

II. PICTURES OF CHRIST

A. Christ in the Passover

The New Testament is filled with references to the Old, and its approach in interpretation gives us a clear license to *expect* to find picture after picture of the Savior—forecasting photographs of His Person, His nature, and His work on the Cross.

The most pronounced is in the Passover. In John 1:29, John the Baptist says, "Behold, the Lamb of God who takes away the sin of the world." Every Jewish listener to his words in that day knew the message: Here is your Savior!

- Even as the blood of the lamb brought protection from the death spreading through Egypt, the Savior saves us from the death penalty sin deals.

- Even as the blood of the lamb brought deliverance from slavery at the hands of cruel taskmasters, the Savior breaks the chains of bondage to sin and destructive habits.

Open your Bible to Exodus 12 and take time to carefully read the directions the Lord gave Moses to relay to the people of Israel concerning the first Passover. Invite the Holy Spirit to show you parallels—aspects of those specifications which hold the seeds of a "type"; that is, a *mark* that is struck or engraved in the picture, which points to a greater fulfillment. According the Scriptures, "Christ IS our Passover!" (1 Corinthians 5:7).

B. Christ in the Tabernacle

One of the reasons Father God so insisted that everything in the Tabernacle be made "according to the pattern" was because so much was meant to foreshadow Jesus Himself. For example: *"Therefore, brethren, having boldness to enter the Holiest by the blood of Jesus, by a new and living way which He consecrated for us, through the veil, that is, His flesh... let us draw near with a true heart in full assurance"* (Hebrews 10:19-22).

Here is a priceless parallel: The sacrifice of Christ on the Cross—including His torn flesh and riven side—depict the fact that *the way to the heart of God has been opened!* Just as the veil separated the ancient worshipper from privileged entry into the Holy of holies—the intimate presence of God—so sin has prohibited our approach. But Jesus' death for us has torn the veil asunder: the Tabernacle picture teaches us clearly that God is saying, “Draw near to me! You can come now—there are no obstacles !”

Take time when reading or listening to the Book of Exodus. As the details of the Tabernacle’s form and contents are described, what pictures of our Lord might be seen...

...in the blood of the sacrifices?

...in the water of the laver?

...in the lampstand?

...in the table of shewbread?

...in the altar of incense?

(These are all shown later in this study guide, but this is your invitation to discover them for yourself, if you wish.)

C. H. MacIntosh, a scholar from the later 19th century, noted a beauty in the repeated directive that wooden objects should be over-laid with gold in the Tabernacle. He suggested a picture of the blend of Christ’s humanity and His divinity—the wood (the vulnerable and ordinary, as with “flesh”), wrapped completely in the gold (the glorious and the worthy, as with “God”). As the Christmas carol says, “Veiled in flesh the Godhead see; Hail the incarnate deity!”—such “snapshots” of the Savior abound in the Tabernacle, and are fulfilling to discover.

C. Christ in the Sacrifices

The Book of Leviticus opens with a full chapter devoted to the details of how each of five different “offerings” (sacrifices) were to be offered. Each one addressed a particular issue, then removed that encumbrance preventing fellowship with God. They each remind us of factors that block the best God has for us, and each one represents something that Christ has done for us in His Cross—all to open "the new and living way" for us to fellowship with the Father, through the saving work of His Son.

1. <u>The Burnt Offering</u> (Leviticus 1): The key trait of this sacrifice is that it was to be all completely consumed. It reminds us of how *completely and totally* Jesus poured out His soul unto death; nothing reserved..."Thy will be done!"

2. <u>The Grain Offering</u> (Leviticus 2): One of the distinctive features of the grain offering was the fact that a portion of the sacrifice was to nourish the priest who presented it. Here is a picture of how Jesus' death not only "paid it all," but how He also has "provided to sustain." He said, "I am the living bread (grain)..." available for ongoing strength.

3. <u>The Peace Offering</u> (Leviticus 3): This focuses on thanksgiving for the privilege of unstrained fellowship. The blood was sprinkled (atoning for sin), but the meat of the sacrifice was roasted to provide a meal for the celebrants. Jesus died to bring us together—with Him and with each other: He is our Peace! (Ephesians 2:14-17).

4. <u>The Sin Offering</u> (Leviticus 4): The beauty of this sacrifice was in its nullification of guilt—even for *unintended* sins or sins of ignorance. Have you ever wondered if there's anything you've forgotten to confess, or didn't know you did? Has God covered it? YES! "Father," He said, "Forgive them for they know not what they do!"

5. <u>The Trespass Offering</u> (Leviticus 5): This was God's way of calling for restitution—for the

worshipper to contribute to the repairing of relationships or restoration of loss when possible. Jesus has fully covered our sin—but having brought us to the Father ("reconciled us to God"), He calls us to be instruments of reconciliation *by the power of His life within us* (2 Corinthians 5:17-21).

D. Christ in the Red Sea Exodus

While Exodus names a Bible book, it is also a word that describes a full exit being realized. In the case of Israel's release from the land, it was accomplished in two steps: (a) by the blood of the Passover, which defended them against the *power of death;* and (b) by the passage through the Red Sea, which removed them from the *power of Pharaoh.*

In 1 Corinthians 10:1-2, Israel is said to have been "baptized into Moses.... It's a powerful figure of speech; it is also dynamically instructive. In short, they were saved from death by the power of the blood, but they found freedom by following a pathway to life under a new leader.

The analogy is not accidental. 1 Corinthians 12:12-13 and Romans 6:1-4 describe a new believer's baptism in water as "into Christ" and as unto a "walk in newness of life." Everyone who comes to the Savior as the Lamb whose Blood breaks the power of eternal death, is then expected to be baptized in water—both a severing experience and a burial (Colossians 2:11-12 and Romans 6:4). This is the Holy Spirit's means to bring us under the Lordship of Christ's rule and, as Pharaoh's power was broken, He will break the bondage of sin's control and Satan's hold on issues or parts of our life.

III. TIMELESS LESSONS FOR LIFE

A. God's Policy: "No Compromise!"

At first, casual readers of the Bible are sometimes puzzled over the fact that God hardened Pharaoh's heart. "It doesn't seem fair," someone cries. But that happens if several things about Pharaoh are overlooked.

First, he *did* have a chance to become the greatest emancipator in history (Exodus 9:16). While God did harden Pharaoh's heart, it was only after he himself said, "Who is the LORD, that I should obey Him!" (Exodus 5:1-2).

Second, even when he did begin to soften, he not only insisted on negotiating for a "lesser" degree of bondage (see 8:25, 28; 10:, 8, 24), he epitomizes the satanic style of saying, "Go serve God…(a) but not far from me; or (b) don't include your children; or (c) don't really sacrifice (that is, "surrender to God"). But God says, "No compromise!"

Finally, it is a historic fact that the pantheon of Egyptian demon-gods were worshiped in the form of idols that were in every animal form that was involved in the judgments on the land. In short, God demonstrated His will then and now—"I will break every demon's power and set my people free: *sin shall not have dominion over you!"*

B. Breaking the "Slave Mentality"

The wilderness journey is a study of the truth that it is easier to get the slave out of Egypt than it is to get Egypt out of the slave. Make your own study of the number of times the Israelites say, "If we could only go back…We'll be ruined if we stay with Moses!"

- Note what the issue is and what it reflects in practical terms of daily living.
- Note what they say and how they say it.
- Note what God does to demonstrate His feelings concerning such attitudes.
- Ask the Holy Spirit if any of these attitudes need to be dealt with in you—conclusively!

C. Miracles of Magnificence in Provision

There is a literal stream of the miraculous that flows throughout the whole of the wilderness journey. Though the people lust for their own way, murmur against God's appointed, anointed leader, witness the repeated mercies of God toward them and rebel again—God remains fully faithful!!

Find each of the following episodes in your Bible, and make notes of your own regarding what each manifestation of God's faithfulness may speak into your own life-circumstance.

- The cloud that blocked Pharaoh's army from advancing until the sea opened.
- The removal of the army's chariot-wheels when it appeared they might overtake Israel.
- The provision of a means for sweetening impossibly bitter waters.
- The promise of an abiding presence of God's healing power.
- The raising of intercessors to stand firm when a battle is raging where you are.
- The provision of daily manna when there is nothing of any resource within sight.
- The covering of a cloud by day (insulation) and providing fire by night (illumination).

- The springing of refreshing water out of a hard, unbending surface—bringing life.

D. The Timeless Warning Against Apathy

In conclusion, wisdom recommends we come to terms with one of the most incredible facts in the Bible: that a people born of a miracle died without the completion of God's miracle purpose for their lives!

The passing of a generation who started well, but ended poorly, speaks profoundly to our human tendency to back away when God calls beyond our *beginnings* in faith to a steady *growth* in faith. The collapse of the congregation in the wilderness is a landmark event the Bible will not let us forget.

- Study Psalm 95, and see how importantly the Word of God joins a heart of remembrance to a heart of worshipful praise. Lesson: I dare not suppose my acquired habit of praise accomplishes a total removal from the possibility of a rebellious heart creeping in.
- Study Hebrews 4, and hear the call to "enter into God's rest"—that is, learn to depend upon His wisdom, His power, His grace…and "lean not on your own understanding."

The pathway from prison to promise is a sandy, gritty, sometimes deserted one. But if we ever and always keep our gaze on the One who has freed us, and walk under the cloud of His grace and glory—we'll always find provision and power…and in time, we'll arrive at the full dimensions of His promised purpose!

THE LIFE OF
MOSES

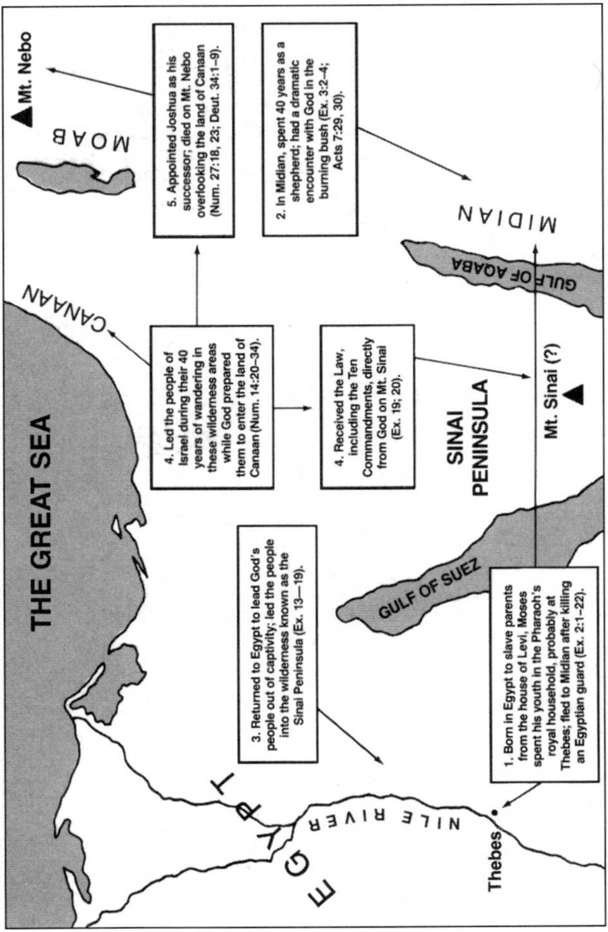

Part 2

THE RELEVANT ANSWERS IN EXODUS, LEVITICUS, NUMBERS, AND DEUTERONOMY

Scott Bauer

Answering Questions and
SOLVING PROBLEMS

Once again, the challenge in dealing with questions in the text of Scripture has to do with a fundamental issue of faith. If it is presumed that the supernatural events described in the Bible cannot happen, then there is no explanation which will suit the doubter. And, if natural phenomena may explain a biblical event, it can either be presumed proof of the absence of supernatural divine intervention, or the demonstration of God's hand at work through natural forces at His command.

This is precisely why the proof of miracles is not in and of itself adequate to lead people to the knowledge of the true and living God. The knowledge of God is a matter of faith. This is not a blind faith which ignores the natural questions and honest inquiries of those seeking truth. It is faith which comes from God Himself (Ephesians 2:8) which becomes the filter through which honest inquiry is pursued. It is a well-established fact that the assumptions a person starts with can, in fact, alter the results and the interpretation of those results as they are observed in the process of evaluating truth. As the text of Scripture is examined, it is these beginning assumptions that may lead to or away from faith in the living God.

Israel's wanderings in the wilderness illustrate this magnificently. Each day the literal physical presence of God was obvious to every Israelite. The pillar of cloud in the day and the pillar of flame in the evening demonstrated God's presence—constantly. Every morning manna (Exodus 16:4) appeared on the ground. The people received this miracle provision of God every day for forty years. It was, without question, the single most dramatic evidence of God's daily concern for His people.

However, it is this same people who complain, rebel, reject, and violate their relationship with God in spite of His intimate and very direct dealings with them at a miracle/supernatural dimension. Whether it is a matter of ingratitude or pure selfishness, it does not change the fact that the miracle workings of God do not produce righteous living. And, miracles can never substitute for faith.

Therefore, as we deal with the great issues of miracles in the Bible, particularly in the book of Exodus and Numbers, the purpose is not to explain the miracles, but to lead people to an investigation of faith and a discovery of God's love and power, which are personally available to all who seek Him.

The Date of the Exodus

Scholars have often debated the date of the deliverance of Israel from Egypt as a matter substantiating or undermining the internal evidence of Scripture and the trustworthiness of the text of Scripture itself. The debate centers on two basic possibilities.

The first possibility relates to the Exodus in or around the reign of Rameses II of Egypt. Exodus 12:37 declares that the Israelites departed "from Rameses to Succoth." It is presumed by some that this proves the Exodus must have happened about the time of Rameses II. Since the dates of the monuments in this city are known, they are presumed to set the timeline of the Exodus at about 1314 B.C.

This late date does not fit the timeline of the Old Testament. It would require the telescoping of the years of the Judges, requiring many of them to have ruled simultaneously. This clearly is not the intent of the chronology of the book of Judges. And, if this date of the Exodus is accepted, the historicity of the Old Testament is questioned and the integrity of the Bible witness compromised.

However, the Old Testament itself offers another timeline for the Exodus. The fall of Samaria is a well-documented date in the ancient world, and it comes after the reign of Solomon in 722 B.C. In 1 Kings 6:1, it offers the date of the building of the Temple—"the 480th year after the children of Israel had come out of the land of Egypt." This date refers to the date of the conquest and the beginning of the possession of the land. Acts 13:20 states the time of the Judges to be "about 450 years"; adding David's rule and the fourth year of Solomon's rule, we approach the 480 years of 1 Kings 6:1.

The argument against the biblical record refers to the mention of the city of Rameses and the historical linkage to Rameses II. However, Genesis 47:11 clearly states that the children of Israel settled "in the land of Rameses." No one suggests that

Joseph and Rameses II could possibly have been contemporaries, as they are separated by the centuries of captivity in Egypt.

Therefore, the historical witness of the Scripture is not threatened by archeological dates which have no bearing upon it. In fact, further historical information strongly supports the notion of the 1520 B.C. date of the Exodus.

Moses was 80 at the time of the Exodus. This means he was born during the time of Thothmes III. Thothmes III would have been an infant at the time of Moses' birth, while Egypt was ruled by his sister, Hatasu. She would have been the daughter of Pharaoh as mentioned in Exodus 2:5. It is interesting to note that no Pharaoh is mentioned—since she ruled Egypt for 20 years, until the majority of her brother.

The Bible timeline is accurate and historically verifiable. The trustworthiness of Scripture bears the weight of intense scrutiny—the Exodus is just another example.

The Red Sea

The route of the Exodus as suggested by the name "Red Sea" requires us to view the crossing of the sea far to the south of where it probably took place. The actual rendering of the Hebrew word "Red" is likely best translated "reed" from the Hebrew, *Yam Suph*. This would describe a place beyond the end of the Red Sea today. However, in the time of Moses, this name is also used for the northern portion of the Red Sea itself—Numbers 33:10.

The actual crossing of the sea most likely took

place miles to the north of where the Red Sea ends today, just to the north of the Gulf of Suez—(the extension of the Red Sea toward Egypt). This would suggest a place near the Bitter Lakes. These lowlands just north of the current boundary of the Red Sea were covered with water at the time of the Exodus. Here, the Lord delivered the people of God from the pursuing chariots of Pharaoh.

There has been some question as to how the Lord could have drowned the Egyptians in the relatively shallow waters of the Reed Sea. In fact, the Suez Canal now traverses some of the area in question, and the Suez Canal Company reports the wind effect difference of the height of the water to be recorded at over ten feet. Interestingly, the same effects have been noticed on Lake Erie with a measurement of over 14 feet (International Standard Bible Encyclopedia, vol. 3, p. 2540).

Therefore, the Bible record of a "strong east wind all night" had the effect of dividing the waters for the people of God to pass through them. This is not beyond the realm of already observed possibility. However, the "dry land" crossing is a feature which truly is a reflection of the supernatural action of God. Though the waters were parted, the soft marshy bottom of the sea would not have dried out.

The evaluation of the miracle on the standards of observed geographical and historical evidence is neither faithless, nor does it detract from the Lord's awesome power. He Who rules over day and night also controls the seas for delivering His people. Some may say the parting of the Red Sea is no miracle—it was for the people of God as they faced Pharaoh's chariots and certain destruction.

The Hardening of Pharaoh's Heart

This question strikes at the very core of what we consider to be the "goodness" and "fairness" of God. Lurking just beneath the consciousness of most people is the fear that God has arbitrarily decided everyone's fate, and our actions are somehow secretly scripted by the Almighty, leaving us no recourse to our final destiny.

This fear is illustrated in the account of Pharaoh hardening his heart. In the passage of the deliverance of Israel from Egyptian bondage is the statement—"I will harden his heart" (Exodus 4:21). This refers to God's action in the matter.

The exaggerated doctrines of **predestination** lead to a false conclusion that Pharaoh is completely beyond his own ability to resist what is taking place in the circumstance around him. Therefore, God has used him as a hapless pawn to demonstrate His power at the expense of a mere mortal.

Nothing could be further from the case. The hardening of Pharaoh's heart is not only known by God in His omniscience, but is also confirmed by the actions of Pharaoh himself—over and over again (Exodus 7:13,22; 8:15; 9:35, 19, 32; 9:7). The references above are all Pharaoh's actions and responsibility.

The hardening of heart refers to the deliberate desensitizing of the human will to the situation. "Dull, heavy, insensitive, stubborn, hard" all describe what Pharaoh did to himself. In fact, his own advisors counseled him that "This is the finger of God" (8:19), and Pharaoh continued to steel himself against God and His people. He violated his own conscience, counselors, and the Spirit of God at work in the situation. It is recorded seven times that Pharaoh stubbornly refused to respond to his own heart's conviction in the situation. It is not a matter of being ignorant or confused. He willfully rejected his own best opinion on the matter in favor of a rigid refusal to acknowledge God.

Later, in the account of the plagues—the sixth plague of boils—God hardens Pharaoh's heart. The Lord simply confirmed the sentence already pursued by Pharaoh as he willfully violated God and his own conscience repeatedly. This does not constitute a divine superimposition of will upon unwilling flesh. It is the consequence of rejecting God.

Illustrated in the life of Judas Iscariot is this same principle. Not only is Judas warned, but he is directly confronted by Jesus Himself at the very hour of his betrayal. The responsibility for Judas' actions is clearly his own (Matthew 26:25). There could be no clearer warning or more loving revelation of the evil Judas was about to perform. Judas witnessed both the teaching, miracles, and evidence of Jesus the Messiah and betrayed Him with absolute clarity of mind and thought—with every opportunity, to the very end, to not follow through on his action.

We are not hopeless pawns in a divine chess game. We are fully responsible, intelligent, and moral beings who make choices to live for or against God. The fact that the Lord knows our decision ahead of time does not make Him the pre-determiner of our actions.

Can The Lord Change His Mind?

The Lord's interaction with Moses in the Pentateuch is extremely unusual. Moses offers insight into his own relationship with God that is so intensely personal and immediate that one sees the intimate details of God's response to His chosen leader. It is in this context that we observe another very challenging passage of Scripture.

In Exodus 32:14, the Bible records the Lord as having "relented" (NKJV), or "repented" (KJV) of His intended course of action with regard to the sin of Israel. The concept of God "changing His mind" or the course of His stated actions excites all kinds of theological challenges. Does God change His mind? Isn't God steadfast and immovable? This text poses a substantial question on the nature of God and His interaction with people.

While Moses was on Mount Sinai receiving the Law directly from God, the Israelites rebelled against the Lord and created a golden calf with their own hands. Unbelievably, they worshiped this calf as the god who brought them out of Egypt (Exodus 32:4). God's instant response was to destroy them and begin a new nation with Moses as a "second Noah" (Exodus 32:10). It was Moses' intercession on behalf of the people which spared their destruction—it is in this context that "God relented."

There are at least two important concepts which govern an approach to understanding this interaction and God's "repentance." First, there are two parallel absolutes in relation to God—He is always merciful; He is always holy. His mercy demands that He forgives; His holiness demands the judgment of those things which are not. He does not arbitrarily administrate either mercy or holiness. However, the heinous rejection of the people in their sin warranted immediate and final judgment in this case. Yet, this was not God's original intention for Israel. He desired to make them a blessing to the whole world as a nation of priests to represent Him (Exodus 19:6).

The Lord's judgment of this kind of sin is wholly in keeping with His nature and character. However, so is His mercy.

Moses' intercession on behalf of the nation (Exodus 32:11-13) releases forgiveness and ends the immediate judgment which would have destroyed the people. This stance is also found in the New Testament, which shows us Jesus as our continual Intercessor before God (Hebrews 7:25; 1 John 2:1). This leads us to the second principle related to the account of God having "relented." God works in concert with the intercession of those who call on Him. He is the sovereign God of the universe; however, He hears the prayers of His people and answers them according to mercy.

Numbers 14:20 is further illustration of this truth. God, once again, has been moved to the brink of destroying Israel. His words to Moses both excite enormous possibilities and, at the same, vest us all with sobering responsibility. "I have pardoned, according to your word." There is no way to interpret these words without quaking at their significance. There are some things in the world which depend on the personal intercession of individuals if breakthrough and blessing are to occur.

Moses' prayers did not change the heart of God

toward Israel. God's heart and intention are displayed back to His response at their oppression in Egypt (Exodus 3:9). Moses' intercession did not create God's gracious heart and intent toward Israel. However, Moses' intercession *released* God's intended purpose for the nation.

In precisely the same way, Jesus' intervention on our behalf spares us from the judgment which is rightfully ours. God's intent toward you and me is clear (Ephesians 1:4)—we are chosen in Him to be holy. Yet, our sin guarantees eternal judgment *except* for the intercession of Jesus Christ before the throne of grace. God's response to Moses does not represent an arbitrary expression of good will; rather, it is the reaffirmation of God's original intent toward His people.

God does not change; He is wholly consistent with His nature. He defines love and holiness. He is the God of mercy and judgment. He is the sovereign ruler of all, and He awaits the intercession of His people to partner with Him in their world. This passage of Scripture only deepens our understanding of God's heart toward us, and our place as servants before Him.

The Work of The Holy Spirit

The most obvious reference to the Spirit of God in these books is seen in God's literal, physical presence in the activities which lead to the Exodus and the later wilderness journey of the people of Israel. The administration of the plagues which eventually bring deliverance from Egypt can be readily understood as the sovereign action of God the Spirit at work according to the divine plan.

As the people left Egypt, the pillar of fire by night and the cloud by day shows us the single most dramatic event of the entire Bible in demonstrating the ongoing presence of God among His people. This visible presence of God in Israel is thrilling to consider. God is present with His people always—and there is the proof! However, it also makes a dramatic point. God's visible presence in Israel did not stop the complaining or sinning of the people. Even as God is visibly present with the people, the nature of man's rebellious, ungrateful, and sinful ways are not restrained. This points to the absolute necessity of the coming of Jesus Christ and our need to be born again by the Spirit of God.

It is not good enough for man to simply witness God's presence in the world around him. The ultimate need is that every person would experience God's presence at work **within them**. Our personal salvation is not simply the update of the Exodus in our life. It is the personal presence of God in us as we receive Jesus Christ by faith. What could not be accomplished by the Spirit of God **among** the people of Israel in the wilderness, can be accomplished **in us** by the Holy Spirit.

The direct reference to the Spirit of God in these books refers to the Lord "filling" (Exodus 31:3), or enabling an individual for a task (Exodus 35:31). In the case of Balaam, the wicked prophet who attempted to curse God's people, the Holy Spirit "came upon him" and he began to prophesy (Numbers 24:2). In preparing Joshua to share in the leadership responsibilities with Israel, Moses is told to "Take Joshua…in whom is the Spirit."

The concept of the present, active work of the Holy Spirit within the individual is clearly present in the Pentateuch. God is directly involved in the lives of His people. From artisans to leaders, God empowers His people uniquely for service they are to render to Him. In the case of Balaam, this work of the Spirit in prophecy obviously had no impact on his life, character, or evil intentions. This is curiously different from the New Testament's understanding of Holy Spirit's work in people.

There is another dimension of the work of the Holy Spirit which is present in these books, though it is not specifically referenced as such. This work of the Spirit can be identified by the way individuals respond to the challenges around them.

Shiphrah and Puah (Exodus 1:17) rejected the orders of Pharaoh to murder newborn Israeli boys as their mothers were giving birth. These midwives "feared God," and they were rewarded by the Lord for their faithfulness.

Moses was fortified to go before Pharaoh and his court to demand the release of God's people. Not only did Moses prophesy each plague, but the whole dimension of his leadership bears the traits of a unique grace and presence of God.

Caleb and Joshua (Numbers 13:30; 14:6-9) brought a dissenting report from the other spies sent to the Promised Land. They were moved by faith to take the land and believe God. Interestingly, when God judged the people for their faithlessness and complaint concerning their resistance to move to the Promised Land—the other spies (who brought a faithless report) perished in the judgment (Numbers 14:37). Joshua and Caleb were not only spared, but they entered the Promised Land with the generation which was born in the wilderness. Those who believe God and act by faith according to what God shows them are rewarded. The consequences for rejecting are obvious as well.

There are those who stubbornly resist God and the work of the Holy Spirit in these books. Pharaoh may be the ultimate picture of the stubbornness before God. Aaron's leadership in the event with the golden calf (Exodus 32:5) is dumbfounding, based on all he witnessed of God's power. Nadab and Abihu, the sons of Aaron, violate the terms of their priesthood offering "strange fire" to the Lord and are judged for it (Leviticus 10:1-2). Aaron and Miriam speak against Moses and his leadership and are smitten with leprosy (Numbers 12:10). Korah leads a rebellion among the people against Moses (Numbers 16:1-2), and God personally destroys him and his family (Numbers 16:31-35).

Clearly, God's Spirit was at work in the lives of these individuals. Resistance to God always brings destruction; response to God's Spirit always brings blessing. God has never changed His ways with people. Those who open to Him by faith, and live accordingly, experience His best. The others are held accountable for their rejection of Him.

THE PLAN OF THE
TABERNACLE

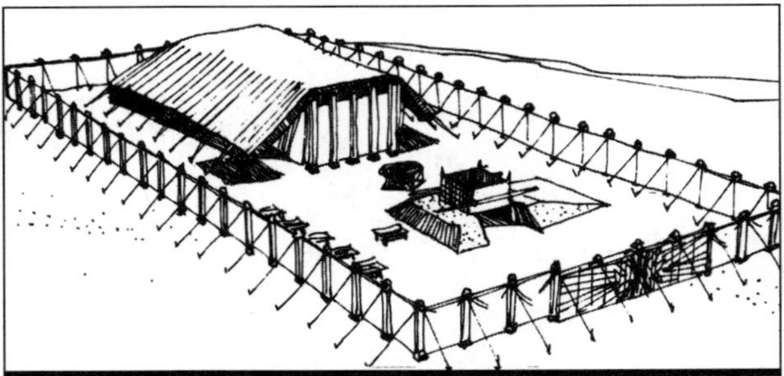

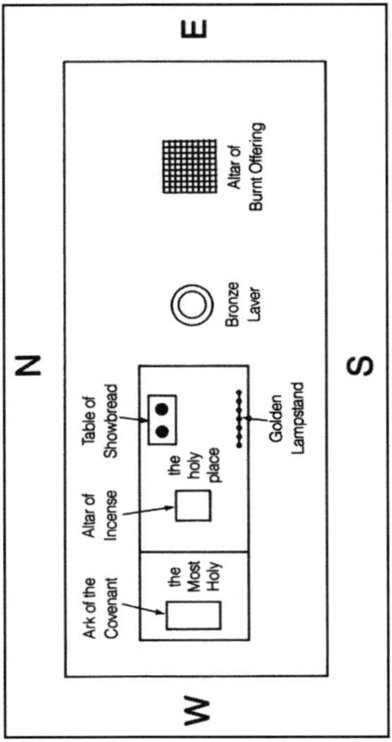

The tabernacle was to provide a place where God might dwell among His people. The term *tabernacle* sometimes refers to the tent, including the holy place and the Most Holy, which was covered with embroidered curtains. But in other places it refers to the entire complex, including the curtained court in which the tent stood.

Part 3

PRACTICAL WISDOM FROM EXODUS, LEVITICUS, NUMBERS, AND DEUTERONOMY

Jack Hamilton

Holy Living in a
PROFANE WORLD

That people can have a relationship with the Almighty God is absolutely amazing. Just think about it: the Eternal fraternizing with the created; the Immortal interacting with the mortal. And the most astounding of all is the Holy engaging with the profane. It is the entanglement of the Holy with the profane that is pointedly addressed in this section of the Bible.

In order to truly appreciate this difference, there is a need to define terms.

The definition of **holy** is "that which is perfect, good, righteous, and whole." This attribute is best exhibited in God Himself. **God is Holy!** It is His testimony of His own person, "I the LORD your God am holy" (Leviticus 19:2). This means that He is separated from sin and devoted to good. Consequently, there is both a relational quality (separated from) and a moral quality (separated from sin and devoted to good) to the phrase "God is holy."

The idea of wholeness is also contained in this definition. The irreducible moral attribute of God is His holiness. Every expression of morality emitted from Him is rooted in the reality of His complete wholeness defined by the incontrovertible statement that God is holy.

In contrast, the word **profane** means "that which is secular, unconcerned with spiritual or righteous purposes." Being unconsecrated, impure, and defiled are further concepts contained in this word. It is the antithesis of holy.

Humanity lives in a profane environment and state resulting from the Fall (Genesis 3). In spite of this current condition, God's plan is to wholly restore both people and the universe. And this restoration will provide a means for and an expectation of holy living, making possible the interaction between people and God on His changeless terms. This demand of holy living should not be dreaded but should be enthusiastically embraced. God's holiness provides the pattern for people to imitate: "You shall be holy; for I the LORD your God am holy" (Leviticus 11:44-45;19:2; 20:26; 1 Peter 1:16).

The basic idea of holiness is that of separation from all that is polluted, defiled, and deadly. The simplest understanding of holiness is that of loving conformity to God's commands and to His Son. Holiness embraces purity and moral integrity. Holy living does not restrict people from enjoying life's fullest joys. It is a preservation from the encroachments of Satan, sin, and self, nullifying their destructive and deadly purposes.

After being qualified through faith in Jesus the holy Savior, a person's life is changed with regard to destiny and direction. The first hurdle to jump in this race of new life is that of condemnation, which always seeks to disqualify one from living as a holy, whole person (Romans 8:1). The second hurdle is the adversary's accusations that counter the declarations of the Lord concerning the basis of holy life (Revelation 12:10). The third and final hurdle is that of the weakness of human flesh which feeds on the habits and attitudes rooted in the past (Galatians 5:24).

After clearing the hurdles, the finish line is in sight and one breaks the tape, like the Olympic runner completing the race. In order to finish this race successfully, one must get rid of the encumbrances and sin that ensnare, running with endurance and looking to Jesus the originator and goal of this faith run (Hebrews 12:1-2). Simply put, it is living a holy life.

Holy God requires holy living from those who call upon Him. In answer to the cry of humanity, He not only makes people new, He sets them on the path of full and satisfying life. This holy requirement enables people to experience the wholeness of reborn living and preserves the whole spirit, soul, and body blameless and are the reasons behind the holy requirement (1 Thessalonians 5:23).

The focus of this section will be on the initial call of God to holy living, the establishing of practices of holy living that affect spiritual life and community living, and to what and to whom the disciplines of holy living point.

The Ten Commandments

Ninety days have passed since Israel left Egyptian enslavement under the leadership of Moses. The Israelites have already experienced the magnificence of the grace and mercy of God in numerous ways: the preservation of the first-born (Passover—Exodus12); the guidance of the LORD by the pillars of cloud and fire (Exodus 13:21); the deliverance from and triumph over Egypt's army through the opening and closing of the Red Sea (Exodus 14); the sweetening of the waters of Marah and, later, the provision of water from the rock in Horeb (Exodus 15:22-25; 17:1-6); and the miraculous provision of food, manna, and quail (Exodus 16).

These miraculous intrusions should have provided a foundation of trust as the people of Israel moved toward the promised geography of Canaan (Genesis 17:8). Sadly, though, they did not. On almost every occasion, the test of faith in God was failed. God, however, continued to move them into His promise as they repented for lack of trust and obedience. Ahead of Israel would be other opportunities for obedience which would be compromised by their inability to perceive what blessings lay in store for them. Perhaps a written code of behavior would alleviate their confusion.

At the base of Mount Sinai, God speaks to Moses and gives him a message for the people. "You have seen what I did to the Egyptians, and how I bore you on eagles' wings and brought you to Myself. Now therefore, if you will indeed obey My voice and keep My covenant, then you shall be a special treasure to Me above all people; for all the earth is Mine. And you shall be to Me a kingdom of priests and a holy nation" (Exodus 19:4-6). Having given the people this covenant message, Moses has the people sanctify themselves (separate themselves for God's service), along with the priests, and the mountain from which God will thunder the basic laws of life and love: the Ten Commandments or the Decalogue.

1. Trust God only (Exodus 20:3).
2. Worship God only; no idols (20:4-5).
3. Use God's name in ways that honor Him (20:7).
4. Rest on the Sabbath day; meditate about God (20:8-11).
5. Honor your parents (20:12).
6. Do not murder (20:13).
7. Be sexually true to your spouse (20:14).
8. Do not steal or defraud (20:15).
9. Tell the truth; do not lie (20:16).
10. Be content with what you have; do not be greedy (20:17).

The Ten Commandments are easily divided into two statements. The first four, simply put, say, "Love God!" The next six declare, "Love others!" On this basis of God's law of love all the requirements of holy living are fulfilled.

When Jesus was asked what is the greatest commandment of all, He stated that to love God with all your heart, with all your soul, with all your mind, and with all your strength is the first commandment. And the second was to love your neighbor as yourself (Mark 12:28-31). In effect, what He did was to reduce the Ten Commandments to these two.

There is an interesting insight into why Israel responded so quickly concerning their willingness to comply with the commands of the Lord (Exodus 19:7). Up to this time the nation grumbled and complained about Moses' leadership. They were unhappy with the way God was dealing with them. When told of His plan for them they immediately said, "All that the LORD has spoken we will do" (Exodus 19:8). Rather than rely on God's grace and mercy, Israel accepted the law as the means to please God. Assuming responsibility for keeping the whole law, they became guilty of violating it all. The Ten Commandments underscored the sin flaw that prevented them from keeping their vow of compliance.

Human pride always makes people think that God can be appeased by performance. The Ten Commandments expose this faulty thinking, and the resulting guilt is compounded by the failure of people's efforts to keep these basic commands. Breaking one point of demand makes a person guilty of violating the whole (James 2:10). Why then were these commandments given if they are not the means of salvation? The commandments were given to teach people of their inability to save themselves and to bring them to God by trusting in His ability to perform His promise (Galatians 3:24).

A. God's Purpose for My Life (Exodus 19:5-6).
   1. Obedience to His word: *"Obey My voice."*
   2. Faithfulness to His promise: *"Keep My covenant."*
   3. Intercession with authority: *"A kingdom of priests."*
   4. Authentic service: *"A holy nation."*

B. God's Processing of My Life (Exodus 20:1-17).
   1. True Worship: *"Love God."* (verses 1, 11).

2. True Witness: *"Love your neighbor."* (verses 12-17).

The Tabernacle

God is invisible. He cannot be seen by natural eyesight nor can He be visualized by the imagination. And He has prohibited the construction of some icon to represent His person. It is a vain exercise to utilize idols to facilitate worship of God who is Spirit (John 4:24). Yet there were always phenomena associated in His encounters with people—bright glory, clouds, fire, thunder, unusual wind, and many other forms of phenomena. God is none of these, but they are witnesses of His presence.

There seems to be a deep seated need in people to have some material form that will promote worship. Identifying a site where God could be met, and decorating that place to stimulate the expressions of the soul, were common actions of people in the Bible and, they are today, too. God does not view this need as a flaw. By giving Moses instructions on the construction of the Tabernacle, God was saying that He would accommodate their need for a place of His presence. In Exodus 25:8, the Lord states, "And let them make Me a sanctuary that I may dwell among them."

The Tabernacle was the focal point of the encampments of Israel. It was the testimony of God's presence which brought great relief to the people. It was also the place where the people came to purify themselves through offerings and sacrifices.

The Tabernacle had a prophetic purpose too. The activity in and accouterments of the Tabernacle pointed to the ultimate sacrifice that would once and for all finish with the question of sin. Jesus Christ was that final sin offering that makes possible the presence of God in the heart of the individual.

The Tabernacle area had three main parts: the **Outer Court**, the **Holy Place**, and the **Holy of Holies**.

The Outer Court was a fenced rectangle, 150 feet long by 75 feet wide. Here the invitation to meet with God was made. "Whosoever will may come" was the message of this area. Upon entering this court, the **Brazen Altar** was first encountered. Here the sacrifices and burnt offerings were made. A perpetual fire was maintained (Leviticus 6:9) that allowed people to come to the LORD at any time and make atonement for sin. This altar pointed to Christ, who would be the final sacrifice for sin. His work would atone for sin by removing its power once and for all (Hebrews 10:10-14).

The **Laver of Water** was also placed in the Outer Court. Here the priests washed themselves before entering the Holy Place. Cleansing was required before service to God could be performed by the priest. Through Christ today, all believers are priests of God. They must remember, however, that their role as priests was not secured through their effort but by the "washing of regeneration and the renewing of the Holy Spirit" (Titus 3:5).

The **Holy Place** was the first room of the Tabernacle proper. There were three articles of furniture in this room that signified the presence of God and pointed to Christ.

First, was the **Table of Showbread**. Twelve

cakes set on the table represented the people of God looking to Him for sustenance. Jesus declares Himself to be the Bread of Life, and He is God's provision for our daily strength (John 6:48-51).

Next was the **Golden Lampstand**. This was an elaborately wrought seven-branched *menorah*. At the top of each branch was a container of olive oil and a wick. Once lit, the light was never to be extinguished. The light was another symbol of God's presence, guidance, and revelation. The Lampstand represents Jesus who said, "I am the light of the world. He who follows Me shall not walk in darkness, but have the light of life" (John 8:12).

Finally, there was the **Altar of Incense**. Here, fire was taken from the Brazen Altar and placed on this inner Altar, incense was applied, and a sweet smelling aroma resulted. It was a symbol of worship and intercession. This was a daily ministration of the priests before the LORD, and represents a type of Christ's intercession for believers in the Christian era (Hebrews 7:25).

The second room of the Tabernacle was called the **Holy of Holies**. It was separated from the Holy Place by a beautifully woven veil of linen with blue, purple, and scarlet yarn. The veil hung from ceiling to floor. In this fifteen-foot-square inner sanctuary was placed the **Ark of the Covenant**. It was a box made of acacia wood, 45 inches long, 27 inches wide, and 27 inches high. Mounted on the top were two carved cherubim (angelic creatures) facing each other with wings outstretched. Between them was placed the Mercy Seat, a slab of gold that covered the entire lid. Inside the Ark of the Covenant were two stone tablets upon which the Ten Commandments were written, a golden pot of manna, and the rod of Aaron which had budded.

Once a year, on the Day of Atonement, *Yom Kippur*, the high priest could enter the Holy of Holies and sprinkle the blood of the sacrifice on the Mercy Seat. When this was done, the sins of the people were atoned for and they were considered not guilty of their sins.

There is much that points to Jesus in this special place. The cherubim remind us that forgiveness of sin is an act that comes from heaven. The blood on the Mercy Seat declares that if it were not for God's mercy, no one could be saved. Mercy alone, however, is not enough. Justice had to be served as well, and it was the blood that met the justice requirement (Leviticus 17:11). The blood of Jesus is the final and complete act of propitiation (satisfaction of divine judgment). The tablets of Law are fulfilled in Christ, the pot of manna represents Christ our sustenance, and the budding rod symbolizes Christ who makes the dead alive with the promise of eternal hope.

The Tabernacle filled the need for a meeting place with God. It also afforded opportunity for meeting God's standard for living and pointed to faith in the Messiah (Jesus Christ) who would make it possible for each individual to be a temple of the Spirit of God.

A. The Tabernacle and My Soul (Exodus 25:1-27:21; 36:8-40:38).
    1. The place of sacrifice (Romans 12:2).

2. The place of worship (Philippians 3:3).

B. The Tabernacle and My Salvation (Exodus 25:10-22).
   1. The place of consecration (Hebrews 10:19-20).
   2. The place of expiation (Romans 3:23-26).
   3. The place of propitiation (1 John 2:1-2).

C. The Tabernacle and My Service (Exodus 37:10-29).
   1. Service is dependent on God (Table of Showbread—John 15:5).
   2. Service offers light to others (Lampstand—Matthew 5:14-16).
   3. Service is an act of worship (Altar of Incense—Matthew 10:40-42).

D. The Tabernacle and My Savior (Exodus 25:10-22; 36:1-9).
   1. He came from heaven (Cherubim—John 1:1-14).
   2. He offers mercy to all (Mercy Seat—Ephesians 2:4-5).
   3. He gave His life for others' sin (Blood—Ephesians 1:7)

The Offerings

Fellowship with God is demanding. A person cannot be casual about it, for God is holy. There is a protocol for interaction between man and God. The unfortunate reality that people face is that sin has created a huge dilemma for them. God cannot be engaged on human terms. His standard is the criteria that must be met. Since sin disqualifies, it would appear that humans are without means to meet God (Romans 3:10-18, 23). God, on the other hand, initiates contact with people and provides the way of dealing with sin in order that man can live in relationship with Him.

In the book of Leviticus, it is recorded that God sets up a series of offerings that allow fellowship between Him and man. The instituted offerings are temporary until God provides the ultimate offering that incorporates all that the Levitical offerings provided. His only begotten Son is this once-and-for-all offering. Faith in Christ not only allows people to approach God, but makes it possible to become part of His family (John 1:12).

These offerings provided personal atonement. Sin may be forgiven, but it demands payment (Romans 6:23). There can be no fellowship with God until sin is dealt with according to His dictates. That means only an acceptable sacrifice could be offered. It was established by God that "without the shedding of blood there is no remission" (Hebrews 9:22; cf. Leviticus 17:11). The innocent and perfect would be the substitute for the guilty and defiled. This system of appeasement was completely fulfilled by Jesus Christ. People can now have fellowship with God because of the eternal power of the blood of Christ (1 John 1:7).

The Feasts

People are prone to forget important events unless something is established to maintain their remembrance. In order to stimulate Israel's commitment to God, He proclaimed that the nation would observe eight feasts to recount His righteous acts among them. They would also remind the people of the nature and character of God. While offerings provided the blood that saved and forgave, the feasts were times of drawing near to God and acknowledging that people are sustained by Him. The list of these feasts is contained in Leviticus 23.

The most common of these feasts was the weekly **Sabbath** observance. This time was called a holy convocation and was to be observed on the seventh day. Setting aside this day unto the LORD was the means of recognizing His place in the life of every individual of the nation.

The **Passover** is next listed. It was established to remember the time of slavery and the miraculous deliverance of God. It is still celebrated annually and centers around a meal of remembrance and promise. It was while observing the Passover seder that Jesus established the Communion Table that is to remind believers that He has provided full deliverance from sin (Matthew 26:26-28).

Immediately following Passover was a seven-day period called the **Feast of Unleavened Bread**. Prior to Passover, all leaven had to be removed from the household, and for the next week only unleavened bread was to be eaten. Leaven represents a type of sin. Therefore, by removing it from the house, people renounced sin and declared their dependence on God for both salvation (Passover) and preservation. It is similar to what the Holy Spirit reminds believers about the Communion observance in 1 Corinthians

11:27-28: they are not to participate in an unworthy manner and are to examine themselves.

The next feast is called **Firstfruits**. It was to be observed fifty days following Passover. This celebration was also called the Feast of Pentecost because of the time it was held. It was primarily a harvest festival where thanksgiving was expressed to God for the harvest. It was during this time that God poured out His Spirit upon the Church, giving it power for witnessing and equipping them to bring in a harvest of souls (Act 2:1-4).

The **Feast of Trumpets** was to be observed in the autumn. It began a time of introspection. Called *Rosh Hashanah*, the observance called for the blowing of trumpets and the offering of sacrifices. It was a reminder when God will call all His people together and Jesus will establish His Kingdom on the earth, for the voice of the archangel and the trumpet of God will usher in that glorious age (1 Thessalonians 4:16-17).

The **Day of Atonement** is the most solemn of the observances. It is marked by fasting, humbling before God, and great reverence. On this day the high priest made atonement for his own sin, then entered the Holy of Holies and sprinkled the blood on the Mercy Seat to atone for the sins of the nation. The blood covered all the sins, failures, and weaknesses of the people, and God's relationship to them was reaffirmed. The final Day of Atonement took place on Calvary. There Jesus was both sacrifice and priest. He shed His blood and presented it as the final atonement for sin. His atonement did not just cover sin—it took sin away (Hebrews 10:10-22).

The **Feast of Tabernacles** was the final of the annual feasts to be kept. For seven days the people of Israel remembered the way of temporary life in the wilderness. They made booths covered with branches and heard the reading of the Law. It commemorated the faithfulness of God in caring for them and bringing them into the promise of a permanent settlement. Believers in Christ need to be reminded that they are only pilgrims on this earth and that Jesus has provided for an eternal home in the heavens for them (John 14:1-3).

Finally, a **Year of Jubilee** was established. Every fiftieth year, on the Day of Atonement, a trumpet was blown to inaugurate a year of Jubilee. During this year-long observance, the land was not tilled, Hebrew slaves were freed, and homeland plots were restored. With the blast of the Shofar, liberty was proclaimed throughout the land. Christ Jesus has set the slave to sin free (Romans 6:22), and the believer is admonished to live in this liberty (Galatians 5:1).

By observing these eight feasts, Israel was reminded that they were living in relationship to a Holy God, and their compliance to these special times kept this miracle ever before them. Because Christ has fulfilled all the requirements of the Law and Prophets (Matthew 5:17), the feasts have served their purpose. As believers observe His triumph at the Table of Communion, they are remembering the Lord's sacrifice and looking for His return (1 Corinthians 11:26).

The Holy Codes

The call to holiness affected every part of Israel's

life. By the time God established the standard for fellowship with Himself, Israel was tainted. He established the means of their fellowship, overriding what kept them apart from Him. Therefore, God set up a legal code to order relationships and a sacrificial system to repair and restore severed relationships due to sin.

The laws concerning relationship with Him were expanded to include things that guided them in their contact with the environment, animals, and each other. Holiness required an awareness of God's presence in all aspects of daily living.

Certain animals were not to be eaten for food. Dietary laws were set forth to promote health. To become sick and weakly from improper diet would make a person less than whole, and being holy required physical wholeness (Leviticus 11:44-47).

Childbirth was to be celebrated. God gave children to families. Therefore, when the male child was born, he was to be circumcised eight days later. There were two reasons for this practice—first, as a sign of covenant relationship with God; second, for hygienic purposes. The mother was to be rested, and then she was to bring an offering to God as an act of purification and thanksgiving (Leviticus 12).

Since health was a principal community issue, God gave laws concerning things like leprosy and bodily discharges (Leviticus 13:1-15:33). The codes were given to stop the transmission of disease through the fluids of the body. Today such knowledge is now being propagated as a means of preventing many forms of sickness and disease.

Sexual perversion is a common human fault.

God gave regulations concerning sexual practices to prevent the sad consequences to a person's spiritual, psychological, and physical well being. God ordained the sexual relationship and confined its expression to marriage (Hebrews 13:4). The violation of sexual restrictions compounds life and pushes one into practices of perversion. Sex outside of marriage, adultery, incest, homosexuality, and bestiality all defile the individual. God's prohibitions are not meant to constrict sexual fulfillment, but to order its practice for the highest good of men and women (Leviticus 18). By submitting to God's counsel in sexual matters, things like rape, pornography, sexually transmitted diseases, and unwanted pregnancies would be stifled.

You Be Holy

All of these codes were meant to protect Israel from the influences of their past practices and the pagan cultures surrounding them. The One who called them out and delivered them from their oppressors had a magnificent purpose for them. God separated them from the defiling elements and provided a means for holy living so that Israel might stay in touch with the LORD who is holy.

Many of the same challenges face the people of God today. Humans fall into traps that compromise their morality and separate them from God. In Christ, the Father has provided salvation from sin and its defilement. He has called the believer to be holy and gives the power to live free from the bondage of the weak and beggarly elements of the world (Galatians 4:9). He promises that He will be our Father and we will be His sons and daughters as we separate ourselves from the polluted and the unclean (2 Corinthians 6:17-18).

"He who called you is holy.
You also be holy in all your conduct..."
1 Peter 1:15.

Additional Ministry Resources

Dr. John Amstutz's CD-ROM

IN THE BEGINNING

makes Bible study easy!

This CD-ROM features Dr. John Amstutz, respected seminary and Bible college instructor and combines videos, charts, graphics, and interactive quizzes to produce a high-quality, informative, and enjoyable introduction to the sacred Scriptures. This cross-platform resource will give you the opportunity to learn in a short, concise, and enjoyable manner about the greatest book ever written.

Half Price! **ITB $9.95**

Works on Macintosh or PC!

Want the Best Study Bible on the Market Today?

The SPIRIT-FILLED LIFE BIBLE *may be what you're looking for!*

The Spirit-Filled Life Bible is a powerful resource for enriching your relationship with Jesus Christ. Faith-filled, prophetic, and Spirit-empowered insights are featured in this one-of-a-kind study Bible. Here, in the light of God's Word, you will discover a Spirit-filled life rich in Godly characteristics. Available in English or Spanish.

Hardback Library Edition: *reg. $37.99* **SFLHB $27.99**

Call for availability and discounted prices for genuine leather editions.

SPIRIT-FILLED LIFE BIBLE FOR STUDENTS

Help your favorite student learn and live God's Word by the Holy Spirit's power!

Softcover **SFLBS $15.99**

Practical Precepts
from the Pentateuch!

THE BLOOD AND THE BOOK

In this five-tape series, Pastor Jack Hayford speaks on the blood, and how it is the central force of truth that runs through the entire Word of God. He shares how the blood established our eternal salvation and created the "New Covenant," and he explains the personal benefit of "pleading the Blood" for our own strength and victory.
(5 tapes) **SC491 $22**

FEASTING UNTO FULFILLMENT

In this series, Pastor Hayford explores the significance of feasting: gives reasons for the institution of feasts; shares insight on why feasts had such a prominent place in biblical times; and then teaches how they can be incorporated into our lives today. (4 tapes)
SC371 $17

Key Teachings from the Old Testament.

LEARNING HOW TO LIVE AGAIN

In this inspiring study of Israel's deliverance, Jack Hayford applies Old Testament lessons to our present circumstances. The ten teachings show how the Old Testament episodes are not only history, but truths which are fully relevant to our lives today. (10 tapes)

SC096 $42

LIVING LIFE TO ITS LIMITS

In this series on the Ten Commandments, Jack Hayford brings life into the "law" God revealed to Moses. The series helps "re-lay" a moral foundation for contemporary believers in their relationship with God and others. (10 audio tapes or 5 videotapes)

SC380 $42

5 VHS Videos **LLLVS $60**

Unveil the Keys to Scripture!

HAYFORD'S BIBLE HANDBOOK

Hayford's Bible Handbook is an unparalleled resource that uniquely unveils the keys to Scripture, providing not only a wealth of information, but also a spiritual stimulus that will encourage your faith and service to Christ.

It unlocks Scripture with:

- Illuminating surveys of each book of the Bible.
- Helpful illustrations, time lines, maps, and charts.
- A complete Visual Survey of the Bible.
- An Encyclopedia Dictionary with over 1,300 entries that address subjects of particular interest to Spirit-filled believers.

This guide opens the riches of Scripture with a unique focus on practical ministry in the Holy Spirit's power—all to deepen your life in Christ. *reg. $24.99* **HBH $22.99**

This guide will open the riches of Scripture and deepen your life in Christ!

ORDER FORM

Qty.	Item	Code	Price	Total
______	______________________________	____	____	____
______	______________________________	____	____	____
______	______________________________	____	____	____
______	______________________________	____	____	____
______	______________________________	____	____	____
______	______________________________	____	____	____
______	______________________________	____	____	____
______	______________________________	____	____	____
______	______________________________	____	____	____
______	______________________________	____	____	____

Postage and Handling

$0.00 - $9.99 .... $2.95
$10.00 - $29.99 .... $4.95
$30.00 - $49.99 .... $6.95
$50.00 and up.......... 15% of subtotal
All orders outside of North America
.... $8, plus 20% of Subtotal

Subtotal ________

Add 8.25% sales tax to CA orders ________

Shipping and Handling ________

Donation (Optional) ________

Total ________

Name ____

Street Address _______________________________________

City ______________________ State ______ Zip __________

Phone Number (______) ________________________________

Method of Payment: ❑ Check or Money Order ❑ Visa ❑ MC

______________________ / ________-________-________-________ / ________
Signature — Card Number — Exp. Date

RESOURCES
LIVING · WAY MINISTRIES

14820 Sherman Way, Van Nuys, CA 91405-2233

Please call for prices and ordering information:

1-800-776-8180 • 1-818-779-8480

Please include your remittance (U.S. currency only) with order.
Make check or money order payable to Living Way Ministries.